# Living the Trinity

by

**Peter Adam**

*Rector of St. Jude's, Carlton, Melbourne, Australia*

## CONTENTS



Copyright Peter Adam 1982 and 1986

## ACKNOWLEDGMENTS

I have used the following material in lectures, sermons, retreat addresses, and study groups, and I am grateful to many who have helped my thinking by their response.

The cover design is by Mike Rutter and the logo is by Helen Snaddon.

This booklet was in its first edition dedicated to the parishioners of St. Jude's, Carlton, Melbourne, Australia, with love, gratitude and anticipation: 'that you may be filled with all the fulness of God'. It is a joy to put it out again in a new edition unchanged in content—and the anticipation is being realized.

Peter Adam

*First Edition* February 1982
*Reprinted in Grove Books Limited Edition* July 1986

**ISSN** 0262–799X

**ISBN** 1 85174 031 7

# 1 YOUR GOD IS TOO SMALL?

In *Your God is too small* J. B. Phillips showed us that Christian life and experience can be stunted and misshapen if it is based on an idea of God which is wrong or inadequate.[1] If we think of God as a heavenly policeman, then we live as if God is merely an agent of law and order, whose presence indicates that we are guilty. If on the other hand we picture God as a Father Christmas, we will expect lots of presents and no great moral demand. This idea that a limited concept of God results in stunted religious practice is not new. Abraham's life of faith was a continual discovery that God was bigger than he had imagined. Isaiah's ridicule of idolatry was that its gods were so limited that men imagine that they have to carry them: the true God is greater than men know, and their lives should reflect their belief in this the only God.[2]

Another version of the same problem is found when Christians forget that God is Father, Son, and Spirit, and concentrate so much on the Father, or on the Son, or on the Spirit, that they neglect the fulness of the Triune God. This kind of specialization within God is dangerous, because it results in a stunted Christian life, and because it is wrong to ignore any part of God's revelation. To respond to the Father, or to the Son, or to the Spirit, and to neglect the others, is to have a God who is too small and a practice of Christianity which is too limited.

Certainly the New Testament account of Christianity includes evidence that full Christian experience involves response to the Father, the Son, and the Spirit, and is the result of the work of that Triune God. For instance 1 Peter 1.2 speaks of those who are 'chosen and destined by God the Father, sanctified by the Spirit for obedience to Jesus Christ and for sprinkling with his blood.' Where the followers of God in the Old Testament had learnt that the God whom they worshipped and obeyed was one God, those of them who came into contact with 'The Way' associated with Jesus of Nazareth had their experience of this one God transformed. The language they learnt to describe this new experience referred to the work of God as that of the Father, the Son, and the Spirit. There was a new richness and diversity in God's action which was revealed in the coming of Christ and of the Spirit, and their language about the activity of God came to reflect this change.

This is not to suggest that Christians of the New Testament Churches believed the doctrine of the Trinity in the language of (one) 'substance' and (three) 'persons' in which it was later expressed.[3] But at least some of the language that they used conforms to the idea that God is both 'one' and 'three', and it is that basic idea of Trinity which is used in this booklet. The unity of God was expressed in the fact that their response to Jesus and the Spirit did not draw them away from the Father, but rather helped them grow to a better understanding of the Father. They

[1] J. B. Phillips *Your God is too small* (Fontana).

[2] Genesis 11-25, Isaiah 44-46.

[3] See, for example, 'Trinity' in A. Richardson *Dictionary of Christian Theology* (SCM) The word 'person' has changed in meaning, so I have included inverted commas when using it in its Trinitarian sense.

knew Christ as Lord and the Spirit as Lord, titles significant because of their Old Testament background of asserting the one true God[1], but describing Christ and the Spirit as Lord did not lead them to an opposition to the Lordship of the Father, or a rejection of the Old Testament. Their belief in the threeness of God was expressed in their recognition of the Lordship of Christ and of the Spirit as well as that of the Father; it was clear that the Father, the Son and the Spirit were not just different revelations of the one God, for Christ the Son prayed to the Father, and the Spirit was 'another counsellor', not just another form of Christ.[2]

B. B. Warfield describes the New Testament experience of God in terms of a 'common Trinitarian consciousness'.[3] I am suggesting a milder form of this idea, that these early Christians grew to know the Lordship of the Father, the Son, and the Spirit, and that it was in this three-fold form that their response to the one God in worship and life was shaped. So in 1 Corinthians 12.4 we read that 'there are varieties of gifts, but the same Spirit; and there are varieties of service, but the same Lord; and there are varieties of working, but it is the same God who inspires them all in every one.' C. K. Barrett comments on these words that 'the Trinitarian formula [Spirit, Lord (Christ), God (Father)] is the more impressive because it seems to be artless and unconscious'.[4] Paul here says that the divine work within the Church comes from the Spirit, the Lord, and God, and his argument for the unity of the Church depends on the basic unity of the three. My point is that the divine work is done not by the Spirit alone, nor by the Lord alone, nor by God alone, but by the Spirit, the Lord, and God. So also in Ephesians 1.3-14, the three-fold divine work elicits a 'blessing'. The Jewish 'Blessing' (e.g. 'Blessed be God who gives food to man') expressed a variety of reasons for praising God, but praise was of course addressed only to the one true God.[5] But in Ephesians 1, the praise of God naturally includes 'the God and Father of our Lord Jesus Christ', the Christ in whom salvation is achieved and in whom it will be fulfilled, and the Spirit who is the present part of this inheritance.[6]

The three-fold activity of God not only is part of the reality of the Church and thus the subject of praise, but also shapes the prayer of the Church. For example in 2 Corinthians 13.14 we read 'The grace of the Lord Jesus Christ, and the love of God, and the fellowship of the Holy Spirit be with you all.' A prayer which only desires the blessing of the Father, or of the Son, or of the Spirit, is incomplete by itself, though it is not less valid for that reason! It must be complemented in the rest of the prayer of the Church by the request for the work of the God who is Father, Son, and Spirit, of which this prayer in 2 Corinthians is such a popular example. For spiritual desire which neglects 'part' of God

[1] Isaiah 45.18-25, Mark 12.35-37, 1 Cor. 8.4-6, 2 Cor. 3.17, Phil. 2.1-11.
[2] These sentences are intended to reject Tritheism (the idea of three gods) and Modalism (the idea that one god appeared in three different ways).
[3] B. B. Warfield 'The Trinity in the New Testament' in *Biblical Foundations.*
[4] C. K. Barrett *Commentary on 1 Corinthians* (A. & C. Black) p.284.
[5] G. B. Caird *Paul's Letters from Prison,* pp.32, 3.
[6] Ephesians 1.3, 4.4-10, 13, 14.

expresses its 'too small' view of God in limited prayers and limited actions.

The same desire for the work of the Triune God is found in more developed form in the prayer in Ephesians 3.14-19. The prayer is addressed to the Father, that 'he may grant you to be strengthened with might through his Spirit in the inner man and that Christ may dwell in your hearts through faith.' Thus you will be 'rooted and grounded in love', will have power to comprehend 'what is the breadth and length and height and depth and to know the love of Christ which passes knowledge', and will be 'filled with all the fulness of God.' The work and experience of the Father, the Spirit, and Christ is the means by which believers may begin to be filled with all the fulness of God. It is through knowledge of the Triune God that the immensity of God's plan and love can be known; the fulness of God's life is found in those who know the Father, the Son, and the Spirit.

The last section of the New Testament to which I want to refer at this point is John 14.16-24. The background to the theme of these verses is found in the Old Testament idea that God dwells with and in his people.[1] John 14 begins with reference to the disciples going to dwell with the Father in 'dwelling-places' prepared by Christ; in verses 16-24 we have the complementary idea of the disciples being 'in-dwelt' by God. In the future they will go to be at home in God's house: in the present God makes his home in them. How does God dwell in his people? In verses 16 and 17 Jesus, who is soon to leave the disciples, says: 'I will pray the Father, and he will give you another Counsellor, to be with you for ever, even the Spirit of truth.' But we should not make the mistake of thinking that the Christian experience of the indwelling God is of a present Spirit, but absent Father and Son. In verse 18 we read 'I [Jesus] will not leave you desolate, I will come to you', and in verse 23 'if a man loves me [Jesus], he will keep my word, and my Father will love him, and we will come to him and make our home with him.' So the indwelling God is the Spirit, the Son, and the Father. This is, of course, a fuller picture of the indwelling God than the common views that Christians are indwelt by the Son, or by the Spirit. It is God himself in his Triune fulness who dwells in men, and in John 14 the disciples are being invited to come to this fulness of knowledge of the indwelling God.

I have tried to show that part of the reason for the richness of New Testament Christianity comes from its doctrine of God, its response to God as Father, Son, and Spirit. It was this varied experience of God which separated early Christianity from its parent-religion, Judaism. The Old Testament doctrine of God was retained, but also expanded by greater knowledge of the God who is Father, Son, and Spirit. The New Testament Church, its life, spirituality, and doctrine, was formed by its experience of the Triune God. It is the purpose of this booklet to encourage Christians today to grow to that same fulness of life and spirituality.

[1] Lev. 26.11-12, Zec. 2.10, 11. See also Rev. 21.3.

Church life today is often limited by an inadequate vision of God, and a particular problem is the tendency to concentrate on the Father, or the Son, or the Spirit, to the exclusion of the others. I hope to show that this is to suffer from the problem of a God who is 'too small', and that fulness of life in God is only found in response to the one God who is Father, Son, and Spirit. We now look at three kinds of Churches, each of which has a limited vision of God, that of the Father, or of the Son, or of the Spirit.

## 2. THREE KINDS OF CHURCHES

### i Church of the Father

The strengths of this Church derive from its knowledge of the Father, and its weaknesses come from its neglect of the Son and the Spirit. Its worship will reflect the characteristics of the Father, the giver of order and stability, the supporter of human society. Its popular hymns will be those which speak of the power and changelessness of God, such as 'O God, our help in ages past', 'Immortal, invisible, God only wise', and 'O worship the king, all glorious above'. The Father is not only the creator and the sustainer of life, he also exercises providential care over individuals and nations, and the celebration of this care will be an apsect of the spirituality of this Church.

Belief in the Fatherhood of God leads to a positive affirmation of the value of all men, and so to a belief in the brotherhood of man. So this Church will be reluctant to be precise about its boundaries, and will rather be anxious to include all men of good-will in its own life, and it will be happy to support charitable causes without applying any test save that of genuine care for humanity. This Church functions well as the church of the local social community, and will probably have annual services for education, local government, rotary, doctors and nurses. In these services the God-given abilities and callings of all will be affirmed. Intercession will be addressed to God the preserver of human society and giver of peace and justice, and there will be prayer for stability, harmony and justice. The rule of God is extended through the co-operation of all men of good-will. Concern for the brotherhood of man throughout the world will be expressed in collections for famine relief and occasionally in political action.

The basic theology of this Church will also be reflected in its use of Bible and sacraments. Sections of the Bible chosen for special services will be those which express the Fatherhood of God and the responsibility of man: Psalm 23 'The Lord is my Shepherd'; Psalm 46 'God is our help and strength'; Christ's summary of the Law as love of God and neighbour; the Gospel parables that speak of human responsibility; and the Lord's Prayer, which is, of course, a prayer addressed to the Father. Baptism and the eucharist will be celebrated as sacraments of creation rather than of salvation. The baptism of children becomes a thanksgiving for physical birth and a reminder of child-like virtues such as trust in the heavenly Father. The eucharist is a thanksgiving for all God's gifts (represented in bread and wine) and an offering of the whole of life to God. Thus the sacraments develop a kind of Harvest Festival theology, and the Harvest Festival itself may take on an almost sacramental significance.

Many of the strong points of the Church of the Father come from its emphasis on the value of the creation, the work of the heavenly Father. People are respected for their good qualities, their gifts, their human potential. Those who contribute to the life of society are valued and honoured. The offering of human life to God is the giving of ability and strength in the service of God in the world. Individual human variety is respected as an aspect of the richness of the Creator's work.

However, this Church has its weaknesses, and they come from a neglect of Christ and the Spirit. If this Church is strong on the idea of creation, it is weak on salvation; if it is strong on the idea of God as the supporter of human lives, it is weak on God's interruption of daily life, confrontation by Christ, repentance and conversion, and the disturbing and bewildering work of the Holy Spirit.

The neglect of the salvation effected by Christ has most serious results in the life of this Church. Its positive emphasis on the value of man is not matched by the complementary truth of his deep need of forgiveness by the death of Christ. This Church will tend to underplay the seriousness of man's predicament as sinner, and so on the one hand it will be guilty of accepting the easy standards of the world, and on the other hand it will not offer any real hope to those who know themselves to be sinners, for a Church which does not preach salvation is unlikely to preach judgment or grace. It will be embarrassed by a sermon on the sinfulness of man, and annoyed at a Gospel which lets prostitutes into the Kingdom before respectable people.[1] At its worst, it offers the affirmation of this life in place of eternal life in Christ, and no hope at all for moral or personal failures.

This Church is unwilling to allow God to interrupt the even pattern of life and worship that he so clearly supports. Christian life is thought of as steady growth: sudden conversion is sure to be harmful: 'decently and in order' is the absolute test of worship, and any interruption of Mattins by the Spirit would produce a horrified silence, followed by lengthy disapproval over Sunday lunch.

Here then is the Church of the Father, in its strengths and weaknesses. It is a good Church as it responds to the Father; it is a bad Church as it neglects the Son and the Spirit.

### ii Church of the Son

The Church of the Son exists in a variety of forms, depending on which features of the life and ministry of Christ the Church is responding to. 'Christ the opponent and critic of society' will produce a radical discipleship entirely dissimilar to that of 'Christ the patient sufferer'. A spirituality that depends on 'Christ the elder brother' will of course be easily compatible with ideas of the Fatherhood of God and the brotherhood of man. The particular form of the Church of the Son is that which concentrates on the Son who is the Saviour, and neglects the Father and the Spirit.

Worship in this Church of the Son is a fervent affair. There is an expectation of God's power exercised through Word and Gospel, a power that confronts, convicts, challenges, and converts to Christ. Worship is both the context in which the salvation of the Son is proclaimed to the community, and also the expression of the community's response. Fervent prayer and hearty singing are the marks of this response to a powerful Gospel. The sermon is a proclamation of Christ the Saviour, and a call to conversion, repentance, and faith in

[1] Matt. 21.28-32.

Christ. Hymns are those which celebrate this salvation: 'How sweet the name of Jesus sounds in a believer's ear'; 'We have heard the joyful sound, Jesus saves'. This theology of the saving God will be reflected in the open admission of sin and guilt, and an acceptance of God's judgment and his highest standards, in the sure knowledge of forgiveness in Christ. Indeed, whereas the Church of the Father's neglect of salvation leads to the forgetting of judgment and grace, the Church of the Son may go to the other extreme and enforce too strict a moral code on its members, and treat people as 'sinners' rather than as people in God's image.

The central themes of the Gospel will be reflected in the sacramental theology of this Church. Baptism will be seen as a sacrament of conversion to Christ, of washing from sin, of participation in the death and resurrection of Christ. The emphasis in the Lord's Supper will be on God's gift to man rather than on man's offering of himself to God, and on that gift as forgiveness and all other benefits of Christ's death. The Lord's Supper is a proclamation by the community of the death of that Lord until he comes; it is a sacrament of the Gospel.

The Church of the Son will have more precise boundaries than the Church of the Father, for membership of the Church belongs to those who confess Jesus Christ as Saviour and Lord. The expectation that this response will be expressed in words as well as in life is a characteristic feature of this Church. While there is the danger of restricting membership to those who can repeat 'O.K. words' and lead boringly conformist lives, there is at least the attempt to exercise that discipline of its members of which the Church of the Father is so apprehensive. A high view of the power of the Gospel to change human lives leads to high expectations in the life of the Church.

The attitude of the Church of the Son to those beyond its boundaries conforms to its belief in the nature of Christianity. Its aim is that of successful evangelism, to bring people to faith in Christ and participation in the Christian community. So while in one way its attitude to Church membership is exclusive (people who do not confess Christ are not part of this Church), in another its attitude is inclusive. For this Church has an active policy of gaining more members from beyond its boundaries.

This strong sense of the Church's boundaries does have its dangers. If the Church of the Father has too weak a view of Christian identity, the Church of the Son tends to become a Christian ghetto, seeing the world only as a disaster area from which souls must be extracted. A strong sense of the isolation of the Church community from its environment often leads to an introspective concern with the internal affairs of the Church community which is both selfish and self-destructive. It is selfish in that it ignores 'outsiders', and self-destructive in its effect on the members of the Church, not least in the adoption of a tight moral, intellectual, and cultural mould which allows for no deviation. The 'over-spiritualization' of life is reflected in the neglect of 'natural' gifts, and in a response to life's dilemmas in purely 'spiritual' terms. It is odd that a Church which believes in the mission of the Son can become introspective and self-centred, and it is also odd that a Church which believes in 'the Word made flesh' can under-value human bodies and personalities. Another regrettable tendency of the Church of the Son is that it concentrates so much on the historical details of the life of the Incarnate Son that it becomes separated from its own contemporary world. These problems are those of a lack of reflection, a natural result of the enthusiasm that is characteristic of this Church.

Another result of the independent convictions and persistent evangelism of the Church of the Son is that it suffers persecution. It is one of the glories of this Church that it is prepared to suffer for its faith, and this witness of suffering is a sign not only of the reality of the faith of the Church, but also of the reality of Christ's sufferings.[1] This Church expects persecution because it follows a suffering Lord, because it knows how to be fools for Christ's sake, and because Christ's servants are not greater than their Lord.[2] Of all the Churches, the Church of the Son is best able to cope with suffering, because the suffering of Christ is basic to its faith.

The strengths of the Church of the Son come from its response to Christ; many of its weaknesses would be remedied if it responded as enthusiastically to the Father and the Spirit.

**iii Church of the Spirit**

The Church of the Spirit is yet another expression of Christianity, and represents a powerful and influential force in the contemporary Church. This Church concentrates on the presence of the Spirit of God in his people, an immediate presence which fills the minds and lives of believers, and empowers them for ministry. The guidance of the Spirit is exercised in freedom and spontaneity, and comes through every member of the Church community.

The signs of the presence of the Spirit are dynamic and public, and the worship of the Church of the Spirit is a celebration of this presence. Worship is engrossing, demands total personal participation, and is an experience of community. The Spirit empowers each member of the Church to minister in different ways to other individuals and to the whole community. This horizontal emphasis on mutual ministry through words and actions is a participation in the Spirit who is present within the Church.

The sacraments of this Church are affected by this theology of the Spirit. Baptism is the celebration of the coming of the cleansing and empowering Spirit, and the eucharist is a meal in the fellowship of the Spirit. It is a family occasion, in which members of the Church family share together, and are bound together by this common participation. Christ as Saviour may be as remote from this understanding of the

[1] Ignatius of Antioch *Letter to the Smyrnaens* 5.1.
[2] 1 Peter 2.18-25, 1 Cor. 4.10, Matt. 10.24, 5.

eucharist as from that of the Church of the Father. If he is present, it is a presence among the people as a reinforcer of community ('We are the body of Christ') or as the giver of the Spirit (the festival of Christ the ascended King). The community emphasis of the eucharistic meal is also found in shared fellowship or coffee, and indeed any common meal or cup of coffee comes to have an almost sacramental significance. There is even the danger that the coffee-cup may replace the chalice as the expression of the sacramental life of the Church—a development of considerable significance, especially in terms of the doctrines of Christ and of Salvation!

While a Church of the Father will be inclusive in its attitude to outsiders (in attitude if not in actions) and a Church of the Son will be exclusive in its membership but inclusive in its evangelistic policy, Churches of the Spirit tend to one extreme or the other. Either the Church is exclusive, and effectively restricts its membership to those who enjoy an identical understanding of the experience of the Spirit, or it is inclusive of anyone who looks 'spiritual', with no theological questions! The extremes of both these policies are of course destructive of the life of the Church.

Emphasis on the power and gifts of the Spirit, which is the glory of this Church, may lead it into mistakes in the area of salvation. If the sign of the presence of the Spirit is gifts, then people not obviously gifted will feel themselves to be failures as Christians and will despair, and people who are obviously gifted may feel that they are saved by the exercise of their gifts, which will lead them to pride (in the short term) and despair (in the long term). The message of the Son is that salvation is by gift, not by gifts; by the gift of Christ himself, not by our use of the Spirit's power.

Whereas the Church of the Son tends to look back two thousand years to the activity of God in history, the Church of the Spirit expects the work of God in the present. The bad side of this is that it may forget the tension involved in waiting for the return of the Son. While life in the Spirit now is a participation in the life of the living God, our present experience of the Spirit is just a 'down-payment' on our future glory.[1] All is not yet understood, put right, healed, or restored, because the Church still waits for the return of the Saviour; only then will the fulness of salvation be accomplished in people and in the world. Whereas the Church of the Father tends to forget that God's promises of salvation have been fulfilled in Christ, the Church of the Spirit is in danger of expecting too much fulfilment in this present age.[2] It has forgotten how to wait for the coming of the King in patience and humility. However, the good side of the expectation of the present work of God in the Church of the Spirit is that it complements the emphasis of the Church of the Son on the work of God in the past (the 'first coming') and the future (the 'second coming'). The Church of the Spirit expects and sees the daily work of God within its community.

[1] Eph. 1.14,
[2] 1 Cor. 4.8-13.

Because the Church of the Spirit neglects the Father and Son it easily forgets the doctrine of creation, that the world is created by God and continually sustained by him, and that he is at work in the smallest and most repetitious detail of its life. When a Church neglects these ideas, it tends to undervalue the ordinary events of life and to believe that God only works in supernatural interventions, and tends to undervalue people's 'natural' (created) gifts in its emphasis on 'spiritual' gifts. The idea that God is only at work in obvious 'miracles' is dangerous because it puts too much value on only one of the ways in which God works in our lives.[1] For the doctrine of creation teaches that God is at work in order and predictability as well as in his 'interventions', in his provision of our daily food as well as in the feeding of the five thousand. God works by plan as well as by spontaneity, an important lesson for the Church of the Spirit, which so easily assumes in liturgy and life that unprepared spontaneity is the only sign of the freedom of the Spirit!

Although this Church emphasizes that each Christian should have his or her gift of the Spirit, it is not an individualistic Church. There is strong emphasis on the common life of the one body, and it may even be the case that individuals may experience considerable pressure to conform to the attitudes of the congregation. However, the sense of corporate identity, of corporate growth in the knowledge of God, is one of the most attractive features of the Church of the Spirit.

[1] A kind of interventionist Deism.

## 3. CHURCH OF THE TRINITY?

I have deliberately parodied these three Churches in order to demonstrate their strengths and their weaknesses. Their strengths derive from the fact that each of them is responding to one 'person' of the Trinity: their weaknesses come from their neglect of the other 'persons'. Whatever their doctrinal formulations, they have limited idea of God. They are right in what they affirm, but wrong in what they deny. It is wrong to concentrate on the Father, or the Son, or the Spirit, to the exclusion of the others, because God is Three-in-One. To ignore any 'person' of the Trinity is to have a God who is 'too small'.

One of the most frequently repeated acts of praise in Anglican worship includes the words 'Glory to the Father, and to the Son, and to the Holy Spirit', and it is to the weakness of the Churches described above that they do not give glory to the one God, Father, Son, and Spirit, in their life and worship. In the words of the Athanasian creed: '. . . we worship one God in Trinity, and in unity . . . the whole three Persons are co-eternal together: and co-equal . . . the Unity in Trinity, and the Trinity in Unity is to be worshipped.' The Triune God is not only to be acknowledged, he is to be worshipped 'neither confounding the Persons; nor dividing the substance'.[1] Because the Godhead is one, the Church should respond to the three 'persons' in one God, and honour and worship the Triune God.

Indeed the doctrine of the unity of the three 'persons' of the Trinity in one God suggests that if a Church specializes in one 'person', and neglects the others, it will not even have a correct understanding of that 'person' whom it does worship. For the only Father is the one who sends the Son and the Spirit (there is no other Father); the only Son is the one who reveals the Father and sends the Spirit (there is no other Son); and the only Spirit is the one who enables us to know the Father and the Son (there is no other Spirit). What is true in doctrine is true in the life of the Church. A Church of the Father which refuses to accept the Son and the Spirit disobeys the Father. A Church of the Son which refuses to accept the Father and the Spirit disobeys the Son. And a Church of the Spirit which refuses to accept the Father and the Son disobeys the Spirit. Churches must continually grow in their knowledge and experience of God, and the God in whom they must grow is the Father, the Son, and the Spirit.

It is of course much easier to have a God who is 'too small', to specialize in the Father, or the Son, or the Spirit. Life is more manageable; it is easier to reach agreement on the life of the Church. The discovery of Trinitarian Christianity involves accepting the need for a greater variety of actions, some of which are difficult to combine. For example, the Church of the Father respects and honours good men beyond its boundaries; the Church of the Son tries to convert them; a Church of the Trinity will have to do both! Or again, worship in a Trinitarian Church will have to be stable and formal (as in a Church of the Father), challenging and direct (as in a Church of the Son), and

[1] The Athanasian Creed (or 'Quicunque vult') is found printed after Evening Prayer in the Book of Common Prayer.

ecstatic and interruptible (as in a Church of the Spirit). How very much easier to limit our knowledge of God! But these conflicting tensions within the life of the Church of the Trinity are the sign of its life, the life of the true and only God. And these tensions will not destroy a Church by fragmenting it, because the Father, Son and Spirit are *one* God, and not three Gods. Indeed growth into the one God is only possible through a whole-hearted response to the Father, the Son, and the Spirit.

One of the most disturbing features of Church life today is that so many popular congregations are those which concentrate on the Father, or the Son, or the Spirit. Is this because limited ideas of God are easier to accept, easier to live, and easier to communicate? There are some popular congregations which manage to combine response to, for example, the Son and the Spirit, but very few have a lively Trinitarian faith and life.

Another congregation may be lively because it has different groups within it, a Father group, a Son group, and a Spirit group. These groups will have very different ideas about how the Church should be run and what aims it should have, and each group will be concerned at the lack of spiritual maturity of the other groups! In this case each group should realize that it is right in what it affirms, and wrong in what it neglects. It should recognize that the other groups also are worshipping the true God, and should determine to grow into a wider understanding of the one God who is Father, Son, and Spirit, perhaps by learning from the other groups. If the Father group, and the Son group, and the Spirit group, each move toward Trinitarian faith and life, they will eventually meet. The place in which they will meet is God himself.

Trinitarian Church life is certainly possible, because God has revealed himself to us as he is: Father, Son, and Spirit. And we saw in various parts of the New Testament that consciousness of a Trinitarian spirituality. I have not yet described a Church of the Trinity, perhaps because it is easier to parody error than it is to convey truth! It would, of course, be possible to draw together all the good features of the Churches of the Father, the Son, and the Spirit, because they will certainly be found in a Church of the Trinity. But true life is not easily captured in words, and I do not think that the way ahead lies in a blueprint of Church life, but rather in the conscious decision of a congregation to discover where it is in relation to God, and to grow in its knowledge of those 'persons' of the Trinity whom it has neglected. This turning to God must occur before a Church can develop a life which is truly Trinitarian.[1]

I have written so far in terms of corporate spirituality, the life of the congregation, because I believe that the great need of our day is not an increase in individual spirituality, but in the development of corporate spirituality. Indeed it is only safe to develop individual spirituality if it is

[1] Theology is more precisely negative than it can be positive. Its negative function is to refute error, but it can never make a positive statement which adequately describes the truth. Error, as the production of man, is more manageable.

done in the context of the spirituality of the larger community. Corporate spirituality was one of the great strengths of the Early Church, the Churches of Luther and Calvin, the Pietists and Puritans, and the Evangelical and Tractarian Revivals, and is a feature of the Charismatic revival in our own day. Spirituality concerns the life of the whole congregation, not just elite groups or individuals, and ministry and spiritual direction which concentrate on the few are sadly deficient. Nevertheless, I think that individuals as well as Churches are called to the Trinitarian life of God, and the kind of test I have applied to the body of Christ is just as applicable to the individual member.

A Christian who thinks of response to God in terms of moral duty, and as the exercise of responsible decision-making after due consideration of all available evidence, is probably informed by faith in the Father. A Christian whose devotion is centred on Christ will almost inevitably think of response to God in terms of careful obedience to the direct command of Christ in Scripture. A Spirit-filled Christian will practise Christianity in terms of response to the inspiration of the Spirit, and of whole-hearted abandonment to that inspiration. Responsibility, obedience and abandonment are three very different ways of responding to God, and they may reflect a concentration on the Father, the Son, and the Spirit, respectively. As there can be tension between different groups in a congregation according to their view of God, so there can be friction between different Christians, Father-Christians, Son-Christians, and Spirit-Christians.[1] And the Christian who tries to combine these different styles of response to God will be in for some tensions as well! Yet of course these tensions are integral to full Christianity. It may be easier to specialize in God the Father, or the Son, or the Spirit; but if we do, we miss out on the fulness of God, and cut ourselves off from other Christians who are concentrating on another 'person' of the Trinity!

Another way of discovering where you are is to ask to whom do you pray. If you naturally pray to the Father, then because you address your prayer to him, your prayers will relate to his character and actions, and this will determine your expectation and living of Christianity. If you pray to the Lord Jesus Christ, then your prayers will correspond to his work and ministry. If your most natural prayer is to the Spirit, then your Christian life will conform to the shape of that prayer. It may be that you pray to 'the Lord' or 'God' without consciously intending the Father, the Son, or the Spirit. However, listen carefully to the content of your prayers, and you may well discover that you do in fact intend to address one 'person' of the Trinity. If, for example, you pray 'Lord, I thank you for dying on the cross', then you are obviously praying to the Son. There is a right way of praying to the one God as 'Lord', and it is not wrong to address the Father, the Son, or the Spirit as 'Lord'.[2] But knowing the Lordship of God involves responding to the Lordship of the Father, of the Son, and of the Spirit. One way of realizing this three-fold Lordship is by consciously responding to the Father, the Son, and the Spirit, as Lord.

[1] 'Christian' and 'Christianity' imply the centrality of the Son. Our general use of these words affects our thinking about the faith, and may cause us to undervalue the Father and the Spirit.

[2] Prayer to 'God' or 'the Lord' as addressed to the unity of God will be discussed below.

## 4. ACTION!

What then is the way ahead for those whose God is 'too small' because they have concentrated on only one or two 'persons' of the Trinity? Action can be taken by a congregation as a whole, by a group within a congregation, by a house-group, or by an individual.

**i Discover where you are.** Use some of the tests described in this booklet to find out whether you concentrate on the Father, the Son, or the Spirit. (You may well discover that you respond to more than one). Test your life, worship, attitude to outsiders, prayers, favourite Bible texts, hymns, and choruses, and see if you can detect an overall pattern of concentration and neglect. If you realize that you have in fact neglected one or two 'persons' of the Trinity, do not despair! Even if you are responding to only one 'person', you are in touch with the living God. Repent of your neglect of the fulness of God, and decide to grow in your understanding and knowledge of the Triune God.

**ii Bible Study.** Raise your expectation of life with the Triune God by studying sections of the Bible which will increase your knowledge of the 'person' to whom you have responded, as well as of the 'persons' whom you have neglected. Study the following; find out what they say about the character and work of the Father, the Son, and the Spirit, and about the response that is expected.

*The Father;* The Sermon on the Mount (Matthew 5-7), the Letter of James, your favourite parables from the Gospels, the Gospel of John.[1]

*The Son:* Acts 2, Mark 14-16, the letter to the Colossians, the Gospel of John, Revelation 5.

*The Spirit:* John 7, 14-16, Acts 2.

*The Father, Son, and Spirit:* John 3.1-16, John 14-16, Ephesians 1.3-14, 3.14-19, Acts 2.

**iii Prayer.** Pray to the 'person' of the Trinity whom you do know, thank him for your knowledge of him, repent of your unwillingness to grow in your experience of God, and ask him to reveal more of his own character and nature, and also to reveal the other 'persons' of the Trinity to you. If you know the Father, remember that he sent the Son and the Spirit. If you know the Son, remember that he reveals the Father and sends the Spirit. If you know the Spirit, remember that he witnesses to the Father and reveals the Son.[2] Pray as a congregation, group, or individual, that God the Holy Trinity will reveal himself to you.

[1] I have not included texts from the Old Testament because it is wrong to equate the God of the Old Testament with the Father. The God of the Old Testament is the one God, later known as Father, Son, and Spirit.

[2] John 3.16; 14.16; 14.9; 20.22; Gal. 4.6; John 15.26.

Try extending your prayer-life by praying to the 'persons' of the Trinity whom you do not normally address. You may do this by using one of the texts given in the Bible study section above. Meditate on it, corporately or individually, and then pray it, using the words and ideas of the text. Or find a hymn or chorus that is specifically directed to the 'person' to whom you want to pray, and use it as a prayer, by singing or saying it. Some suggestions:

*The Father.*
'Father, hear the prayer we offer',
'Hallelujah, my Father',
'Be thou my vision'.

*The Son.*
'Lord Jesus Christ, you have come to us',
'Lord Jesus, think on me',
'Jesu, thou joy of loving hearts'.

*The Spirit.*
'Come Holy Ghost, our souls inspire',
'Breathe on me, Breath of God',
'O Breath of Life, come sweeping through us',
'Spirit of the Living God, fall afresh on me'.

Some hymns and choruses address the Father, the Son, and the Spirit, in succeeding verses. Use them, and consciously address the 'person' concerned. For example:

'Father of Heaven, whose love profound',
'Father, we adore you, lay our lives before you',
'Father, Lord of all creation'.

Of course our prayers need not always be self-consciously Trinitarian, and it is right to pray to 'God' or to 'the Lord' without specifically intending the Father, the Son, or the Spirit, because we may well address the unity of the Triune God, because he is 'one' as well as 'three'. And intercessory prayer is perhaps most naturally addressed to the Father.[1] But knowing God as one is complemented by our knowing God as three-in-one, and praying to each 'person' of the Trinity is a way of growing in our knowledge of the Triune God.

Prayer to the Spirit is probably the most difficult (and the most suspect), perhaps because we find it easier to imagine the Father and the Son in personal terms. Prayer to the Spirit is included in our prayer to 'God', because God is Father, Son, and Spirit. However, the practice of prayer specifically addressed to the Spirit does not have much support in the Bible or in the tradition of the Church. But we are happy to sing prayers to the Spirit (see for example some of the hymns mentioned above), and surely if we can sing prayers to the Spirit we can say them as well!

[1] John 16.23.

The Spirit is described in impersonal images in the Bible (for example wind, fire, and water in Acts 2), and it is easier to address Jesus in the personal image of shepherd than to address the Spirit in the impersonal image of fire. But Christ is also described in impersonal images (for example bread, door and rock in John 6, John 10, and 1 Corinthians 10), so we should not be unused to using impersonal images as a source of devotion and prayer to a God whom we know to be more than personal.

**iv Review your life.** Study the life of your group or congregation, and discover ways in which it might better reflect the life of the Triune God in its worship, its prayers of intercession, its attitudes to people within the Church and outside the Church, its attitude to the world. Decide to extend your response to God, Father, Son, and Spirit.

## 5. THE LOVE OF THE FATHER, THE SON, AND THE SPIRIT

The doctrine of the Trinity is not only relevant to the subject of our response, life, and prayers, it also attempts to describe the way in which the Triune God comes to us. So in terms of God's love for us, it is not just that the one God loves us.

GOD —LOVE→ US,

nor is it just that the Father, Son, and Spirit love us

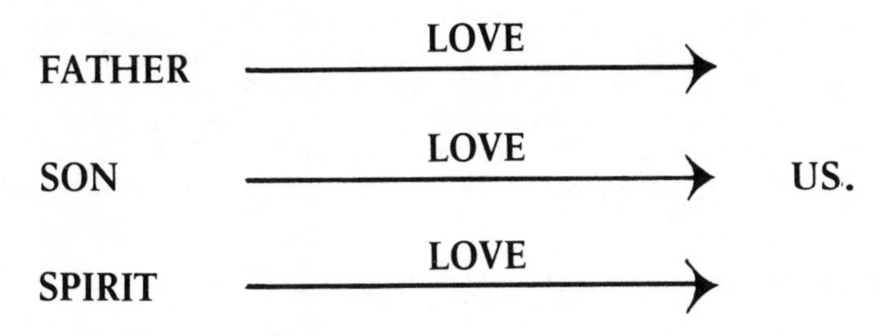


Rather, there is within the life of God a powerful love between the Father, the Son, and the Spirit.

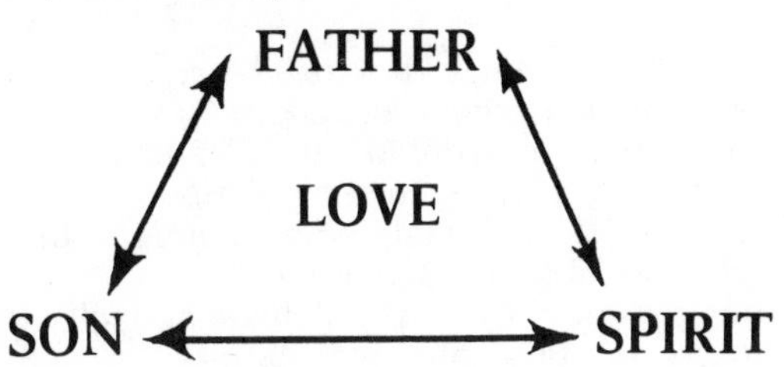


This eternal triangle of love is not exclusive, but inclusive. By the mercy of God, we are brought into the active field of God's love. We are included in the loving life of God himself.

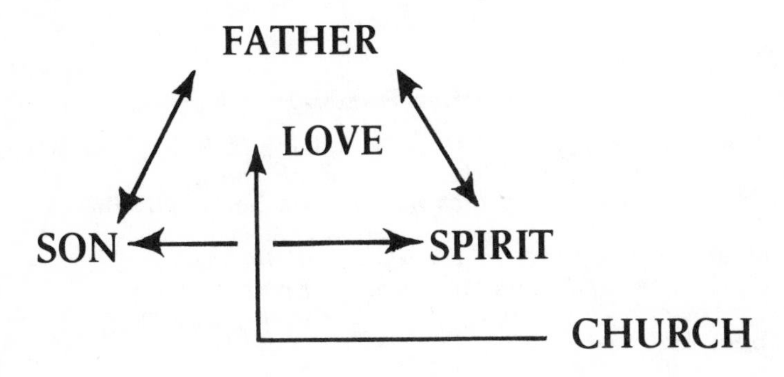

We do not lose our identity or drown in the sea of God's love. But we are included in the love with which God loves himself. The Father loves us in the Son, the Son loves us as a gift of the Father to himself, the Spirit pours the love of God into our hearts.

Life caught up in God is more like relating to a loving community than it is like relating to a loving individual. We turn to the Father, and he gives us the Son and the Spirit; we turn to the Son, and he shows us the Father and breathes the Spirit upon us; we turn to the Spirit, and he shows us the Father and the Son.

Conscious experience of God is only a small part of our life in God, and it would be dangerous to search for a permanent and vivid experience of the Triune God. But as Christian people are aware of the basic orientation of their lives to God, at times a vivid experience, at other times only by faith, so in the same way we should be aware of a three-fold orientation to the Father and the Son and the Spirit, a three-fold orientation which is part of our life in the love of the one God who is Father, Son, and Spirit.

**Action.** Read and pray Ephesians 3.14-19.

> 'Batter my heart, three-person'd God . . .'
>
> John Donne

> 'To God the Father, who loved us, and made us accepted in the Beloved;
> To God the Son, who loved us, and loosed us from our sins by his own blood:
> To God the Holy Ghost, who sheddeth the love of God abroad in our hearts:
> To the one true God be all love and all glory for time and for eternity.'

## Further Reading

T. A. Smail *The Forgotten Father* (Hodder and Stoughton, 1980).
J. Owen *Communion with God* (Banner of Truth)
R. Bauckham *Knowing God Incarnate* (Grove Spirituality Series no. 6, 1983)
J. Moltmann *The Church in the Power of the Spirit* (S.C.M.)
R. P. C. Hanson *God: Creator, Saviour, Spirit* (S.C.M.)
C. W. Lowry *The Trinity in Christian Devotion* (Eyre & Spottiswoode).